PHOTOGRAPHS BY
NEIL LEIFER

SPO

R T S

FOREWORD BY
LANCE MORROW

INTRODUCTION BY
ROY BLOUNT, JR.

CollinsPublishersSanFrancisco
A Division of HarperCollins*Publishers*

In memory of Andre Laguerre,
who saw something in me and gave me a chance.
Merci.

First published 1992 by
Collins Publishers San Francisco
1160 Battery Street
San Francisco, California 94111

Produced by
Welcome Enterprises, Inc.
164 East 95 Street
New York, New York 10128

Designer: Nai Chang
Project Manager: Hiro Clark
Editor: Jennifer Downing
Picture Editor: Daniel Cohen

Library of Congress Cataloging-in-Publication Data

Leifer, Neil.
 Sports / photographs by Neil Leifer; foreword by Lance Morrow;
 introduction by Roy Blount, Jr.
  p. cm.
 ISBN 0-00-255108-X
 1. Athletes—Portraits. I. Title.
 GV697.A1L4173 1992
 779'.9796—dc20   92-13339

Printed in Japan by Dai Nippon
2 4 6 8 10 9 7 5 3 1

Captions to preceding pages:

Page 1: The Astrodome, Houston, Texas, May 1966.
Pages 2-3: (top) Atlanta Braves vs. Pittsburgh Pirates, National
     League Championship Series, Fulton County Stadium,
     Atlanta, Georgia, October 1991; (middle) Collegiate football,
     Army vs. Colgate, West Point, New York, November 1989;
     (bottom) Breeders' Cup paddock, Gulf Stream Park,
     Hallandale, Florida, November 1989.
Pages 4-5: (top) NCAA basketball tournament, The Omni,
     Atlanta, Georgia, March 1989; (bottom) Cycling, Summer
     Olympic Games, Seoul, South Korea, September 1988.
Pages 6-7: Waimea Bay, Hawaii, December 1967.

CONTENTS

Neil L
Ringside   Hollyfield-Foreman
4-19-'91   Atlantic City   your
                            friend LeRoy Neiman

FOREWORD

One morning after a February storm, Neil Leifer and I drove north from Los Angeles on the Pacific Coast Highway. On our left the ocean was quiet. A white fog lay upon the metallic water, which seemed to breathe softly in and out, like someone sleeping.

Neil and I had the road pretty much to ourselves. We talked idly about the perfect crime. We considered the perfect murder for a while, but perhaps because neither of us is particularly murderous, our hearts were not in it, and somewhere just above Malibu Neil proceeded to design the perfect escape. He stipulated an ideal Leifer challenge: the trick would be to get out of a maximum-security American prison. And stay out. And not get anyone hurt in the course of the stunt.

We daydreamed on that for a few miles. The coast highway was littered here and there with rockslides that the storm had washed down during the night from the dun hills that rose sharply beside us on the right. Low-ceiling clouds were layered in a plane like a geometric abstraction across the hilltops. Farther up the coast we saw little mountains poking through the flat white flannel—a Japanese effect, the floating world, a Zen rock garden.

Neil knows something about prisons, having once shot a dramatic essay for *Time* on criminals on the inside of America's maximum-security slammers. The exercise was handsomely done, but un-Leiferlike in its grimness. The prisoners seemed gray and sullen, and if they did not look defeated, they should have looked defeated, considering what they had done to get there. Charles Manson posed for Neil in a prison in Vacaville, California. He was serving life for the murders committed up one of the canyons not many miles from where we now drove.

"It's ridiculous, what they say about Manson's eyes," Neil remarked. "They're not satanic. Not close to it. You can make anyone's eyes look insane if you cut in so close that all you see are eyes."

Neil was driving our rental Ford. His own eyes look like vivid blue marbles and, unlike Manson's, have a great deal of motion in them.

Our conversation became a monologue. Neil's imagination was obsessively and playfully engaged with the idea of the perfect prison escape, and now he unfolded an intricate, precisely timed drama that involved springing an innocent man from Attica through penetration by a TV news crew, which would unwittingly serve as a kind of electronic can opener to pry open the steel doors for a moment. See, the unsuspecting P.R.-minded warden, wishing to change Attica's, er, image, would foolishly allow a major network's morning news show to focus a program on the prison. One of the show's anchors would be admitted with camera and sound crew to interview some of the inmates and guards and, of course, the warden himself.

California slipped by outside our windows. On and on spun Neil's plot—characters sketched, technical problems introduced and then ingeniously overcome, security checks passed, identities changed—Neil's secret being an elegant switcheroo in which our innocent hero (who bears at least a passing resemblance to Neil Leifer) trades places with a member of the TV news crew. He exits at the end of the day under a load of camera equipment, turning in at the security gate the TV crewman's identity tag and motoring off like Toad of Toad Hall when he escaped from a similar dungeon. Toad's device, of course, was to disguise himself as a washer woman.

Neil and I were on an assignment for *Time* that would take us into state parks on the coast where some homeless people were semi-permanently camping: a scenic kind of homelessness. Just as Neil invented the prison break, the denouement of the scenario, the sky over the Pacific coast began to break and shot cathedral rays of sun down onto the wet hills and metal-skinned ocean. The light gave the fog a mysterious luminescence: earth and air glowed, a moment of sweet, unexpected grace. Click.

And Neil, now that he had so elegantly, flawlessly, brilliantly escaped from the maximum-security prison he had conjured, flashed a grin of serene aesthetic satisfaction. A year later, Neil had turned his prison-escape story into a screenplay.

Great photographs have a mysterious life of their own. Neil's often amaze me with their drama, their powerful inner workings. Like Neil, they tend to burst with energy. They usually tell stories—or densely hint at stories. They have narratives compacted within them in that unsettling, metaphysical way that great photographs have. (I think that Neil enjoys it when I write or talk this way, using words like *metaphysical* to try to explain the pictures. I have a feeling that fancy speculations about photography arouse the satirist in him. He may tolerate them when they come from me because we are friends and because he figures that that kind of talk is part of the inevitable price a man pays for having gone to Harvard. "Lance can't help it. You see, when he was young . . ." I was going to quote Susan Sontag discussing what Balzac said about photographs, but for Neil's sake I will try to keep it down.)

Leifer is a gleeful character, I have found. But his energy is never headlong. As I observed when Neil was devising the perfect escape, he brings a sort of focused cunning to his work, a keen premeditation. If his imagination is playful, the technique that is its servant seems to me a street-shrewd fanatic. I have no expertise in photography, but I have noticed that the sheer technique part of Leifer is a superb advance man.

Neil is famous among photographers and editors for his relentless, single-minded pursuit. Once in the pre-glasnost days, Neil went to work on some Soviet officials to get permission to photograph the latest Soviet aircraft carrier in operation. Neil's operating theory is that charm, combined with endless, unprecedented, mind-boggling, supernatural persistence, can pick any lock, open any door, defeat any bureaucracy. He uses a kind of jujitsu to defeat the most massive stupidity and reluctance. But the Evil Empire was more massively stupid and reluctant and bureaucratic than anything that Neil had encountered previously. Fear and vodka, maybe, had the system brain-dead. The role model, after all, was Leonid Brezhnev. Anyway, the Soviets refused Neil. The day after this happened, I encountered him in the halls of *Time*, and he shook his head in amused amazement. "When they say no," he said incredulously, "they really mean no." Anyway, it is my theory that Neil's assault so weakened the Soviet superstructure that its collapse became inevitable, only a matter of time.

Leifer has a kind of genius for ambush, for preparing the instant when all the elements will coalesce—lights, angles, images, nature, and humans performing certain feats at just that instant. Most of the factors, I suppose, are unpredictable, and the possibilities have a tendency to scatter like terrified wild animals and leave behind a million circum-stances the photographer could not have foreseen.

Luck strikes now and then, I guess, but it is an unreliable, some-times vaguely sinister partner. No photographer could make a career of it. When Robert Capa took his picture of the Spaniard on a hillside in violent mid-air crucifixion, at the instant the bullet hit him—one of the defining icons of twentieth-century history and photography—it was, of course, blind chance for Capa, who had just stuck up his camera and fired. It was not such good luck for the Spaniard who was caught in that horrific triangulation of sniper and photojournalist.

Luck comes and goes. I think Neil has unusual foresight—literally sighting things before they happen, imagining them in advance, having his camera ready, just right, when reality comes along. A sort of military gift, it may be. Napoleon once warned his marshals that the gravest sin of a commander in the field is "to form pictures"—to imagine the future circumstances too vividly, for too much artistic premonition leads to delusion, and after all lives are at stake. But since Neil risks killing no one, he can afford to form pictures before they happen. Some of his most famous photographs began with a sort of inventive clairvoyance.

During the Los Angeles Olympics in 1984, for example, Neil studied the stadium, the long-jump pit. He knew that with the camera in a certain position, Carl Lewis sailing through the air would be backlit by the late afternoon sun and that the stands would be in shadow. One problem: photographers were not permitted to shoot from that place on the field. Early in the day, Neil prepositioned his camera, taping down the exposure and focus, and left it on the field. Heinz Kluetmeier, a photographer shooting for *Sports Illustrated* on an ABC credential, was allowed onto the field as a pool photographer and agreed that when Carl Lewis left the ground, he would press the trigger on the remote cable leading to Neil's set-up motor-driven camera, which would then fire continuously, five frames per second. The result is Neil Leifer's image of Carl Lewis in the brilliant energy of world-record flight.

Several years ago, Neil and I were preparing essays (his photographs, my words) for *Time* about the animals of East Africa. Neil once said of his round-the-world Olympics essay that it was not only the best assignment he had ever had, it was the best assignment he had ever heard of. The African trip was the best assignment *I* had ever had or heard of. For seven weeks or so we wandered through Kenya in Land Cruisers chasing elephants and lions and leopards and warthogs and all the rest. Much of the time we depended upon luck and our guides' experience at finding the game. Once, on Don Hunt's game ranch almost in the shadow of Mount Kenya, Neil wanted to lure giraffes back to the acacia trees—Mount Kenya in the background—where he had photographed Kenyan runners Kipkoech and Charles Cheruiyot. Don Hunt laid out upon the ground bales of straw that were laced with molasses—a treat for the giraffes. After several mornings, the giraffes became accustomed to such luxury and came when Neil wanted them, at the magic hour just after dawn.

At that hour, the light of the early sun takes every blade and leaf in profile, and every stripe and horn has a golden brush about it. The world seems to be lighted from within, and the sunlight looks like a soft brilliant wind coming out of the east, blowing morning light across the deep grasses and acacias. In the evening you get another magic light, in the hour before sunset—richer, perhaps mellower, with a scrim of elegy.

Mere staging cannot account for the magic that regularly finds its way into Leifer's camera. I cannot account for it either. The amateur is always amazed when something shows up in the picture that is mysteriously personal: something that is alive with the imagination of the photographer, that in fact proclaims the photographer, has the photographer's personality and soul on it like fingerprints. Why? After all, the surly amateur thinks, it was just a camera getting its button pushed. It still astonishes me, even though the thought is a cliché and I should know better.

In the conception of a human being, the eyes begin forming within the brain. As the fetus develops, they move outward until they become windows through which outer world and inner brain flow back and forth in intelligent connection. So somehow in the picture-making the brain and eye work through another lens, that of the intervening camera, which freezes the instant: the drama and the secret. Vladimir Nabokov wrote a novel in the early sixties called *Pale Fire,* in which a poet named John Shade wrote: "All colors make me happy, even gray. / My eyes were such that literally they / Took photographs. . . ."

Neil's photographs perfectly proclaim the man who takes them. What is his style? I think of Neil's work as a form of bright energy. It is hackneyed to make a mystery look like Hamlet, all dark and broody and inert, the eyes peering out from the skull as from a dark hole. Neil's work, I think, captures more interesting and attractive enigmas. They are full of action, they release energy like electrons firing through space. Something happens. The pictures have the mysterious clarity of the real. Neil is a bardic photographer. His pictures tell heroic stories that tap into primal dimensions of wonder and desire.

Oh, all right: here is Susan Sontag and Balzac. Susan Sontag recalled that Balzac had a "vague dread" of being photographed. Like some primitive peoples he thought that the camera steals something of the soul. He told a friend that "every body in its natural state is made up of a series of ghostly images, superimposed in layers to infinity, wrapped in infinitesimal films." Every time a photograph was made, Balzac feared, another thin layer of the subject's being would be stripped off to become not life as before, but a membrane of memory in a sort of translucent antiworld.

Stealing souls, stealing the world. If this is so, then Neil Leifer when taking pictures is committing the perfect crime.

LANCE MORROW

INTRODUCTION

What I try to catch is a verbal image.

Reggie Jackson, about to retire:
   "I don't want to go on wringing out the rag of ability."

A scout, when Dave Winfield was slumping at the plate:
   "Winfield doesn't trust his hands."

But word-pictures are tricky to come up with in regard to photography. I don't want to find myself wringing out the rag of imagery.

A researcher and I are looking at Neil Leifer's picture of Nolan Ryan looking at . . . what? At the catcher's mitt, presumably, but Ryan's face—seasoned but earnest—suggests an awareness deeper than *there it is: my target.* His face reflects a player who still has a faucet of delivery and knows how to turn it on and off. Ryan's arm is already following through, but the ball is off to the left of the frame as if it is living a life of its own, maybe even looking over the pitcher's shoulder—looking to see where Ryan is looking, so it will know where to go. The pitcher's eye will not be on the ball until it has traveled a good many more feet toward where he has thrown it. Something about the pitcher's trust in his hands, and his arm, has been captured here, because . . .
   "The focus is so sharp!" the researcher says. Ah.
   People take sharp focus for granted in fine photography, but Neil Leifer's focus is arresting. This picture's focus catches the pitcher's focus, in its simple earned faith and impenetrability, and also catches the ball, in its own right. At the park or on TV we see only the pitcher uncoiling and the pitch streaking. In Leifer's picture we see the diamond freshly faceted.
   "Writers can be talking when something happens," Leifer points out, "and they can watch the replay. A photographer's got to be awake, sober—if you don't get it, it's gone. People ask me, 'Can you enjoy an event through the camera?' You enjoy it more, because you've got to focus on it."

The concept of focusing as in concentrating one's attention on something doesn't appear in English until the nineteenth century, after the invention of photography. *Focus* is Latin for hearth or fireplace, and its original English meaning seems to have been the "burning point of a lens or mirror"—the point at which reflected or refracted sunbeams converge to start a fire. A photograph is steady, you can sit and look at it, but it also implies combustion.

I have never seen Leifer not visibly focused. Compactly roundish in build, pointed in his movements and remarks. Hopping and lining things up. This is not always true of photographers—some of them seem sort of drifty, until you look at their eyes.

"I grew up on the Lower East Side in a poor family," Leifer says, "and I never dreamed photography would give me such an opportunity to see the world. I grew up on the schoolyards and was never a *good* athlete—just an average athlete, a shortstop and outfielder in Little League. When I was thirteen or fourteen I started taking pictures for a hobby—started shooting sports, and I lived and breathed it."

He couldn't get field credentials in his early teens, so he got onto the sidelines of Yankee Stadium by wheeling paraplegics in and by bringing coffee to the cops. Concealing one Yashica Mat camera with an 80-millimeter lens under his coat. On his sixteenth birthday he took a now-famous picture of the Colts' Alan Ameche scoring the sudden-death touchdown that won the 1958 NFL playoff—the climax of a game that is often cited as having established pro football as a major American concern.

"When I was starting out, a young, bright, ambitious kid didn't want to be a photographer; he wanted to be a doctor or a lawyer. Now they're coming out of college with degrees in photography. When I was still seventeen my father, who didn't believe in buying on time, broke down and agreed to sign for installment payments on a $450 Nikon with a motordrive, so I could cover the 1960 World Series in Pittsburgh. Dell Publications got me a credential. My heroes, Marvin Newman, Hy Peskin, John Zimmerman, were shooting for *Sports Illustrated.* In the first roll of film, Yogi Berra got picked off second and *Sports Illustrated* used my picture full page—for the only page of color they ran then—for $300, and another one of Mantle, black and white and also full page, for $150.

"*A.*, that let me know I could compete with my heroes. *B.*, it paid for the camera. *C.*, it almost convinced my dad that photography might be an acceptable career."

Thirty-four years after the Ameche picture, Leifer is still hungry but also entitled to some snappy nostalgia. "Jimmy Brown running in the mud—with artificial turf, you don't have those pictures anymore. Now the fourth quarter looks the same as the first. And to get to athletes you have to go through fifteen agents. And television lights things indoors in a way that creates a completely different look. In the boxing ring it used to be dramatic, the light straight down, shadows. Today the ring is flooded and so are the celebrities in the front rows.

The canvas used to be either solid white or a nice light blue. Now ten or twelve feet of the twenty-four-foot canvas is a big Bud Lite sign or Don King's logo. I don't want it to sound like you can't still do a good job, but things have changed."

Technology affects what you focus on. "I couldn't have gotten the Ameche picture if I hadn't been a poor kid with a poor camera—without a long lens I couldn't fill the picture with Ameche in closeup coming through the hole, so I got the lights of the stadium, the mood of late afternoon. Equipment drove the image."

Luck helps drive it. The first Ali–Frazier fight, Leifer and Tony Triolo were covering for *Sports Illustrated,* and Leifer says, "I dream of having the kind of night I had. I'd pick up the 85, it'd be the right lens. Pick up the 50, the right lens. I was in rhythm, in focus—sometimes you *feel* you're getting it. I felt Ali was going to win. Ali would go bingbingbing, I would go bingbingbing. In the tenth or twelfth I felt I'd better shoot some Frazier. In the fifteenth Frazier knocked Ali down right in front of Triolo. I got a page and a half, Ali with his feet up, but you want to get the cover and Tony's was much better; he got it."

A motivated athlete also helps. "Muhammad Ali loves to pose. You can't take a bad picture of the guy. Sometimes people come in wearing all the wrong colors. Ali was always right. The first time I did Ali, in 1964, I was twenty-one and looked about eleven. Ali said, 'I just been with Avedon. Why'd they send a kid? Why'd you put a light over there? Karsh wouldn't have a light back there,' "—and Ali, in fact less than a year older than Leifer, was smilingly autofocusing all the while, as he did a few months ago when Leifer, after helping the weakened Greatest get dressed, shot his all-time-favorite subject with a fiftieth-birthday cake for a *Sports Illustrated* cover.

But the essential drive is the photographer's. Leifer talks Olympians into posing with all the medals they're likely to win before they win them. Leifer goes around the world. Leifer poses Cuban Olympic boxer Teófilo Stevenson with Fidel Castro, and gets a little something extra from El Presidente.

"End of a session, I always have a picture taken with the subject. Eddie Adams, a well-known photographer, had posed with Castro, both wearing duckhunting outfits and carrying guns. I'd made a bet I could get a better picture. Castro lighting my cigar. On the other side of the camera are my assistant, Tony Suarez, taking the picture, and half the generals in the Cuban army. I don't smoke. I can't get the cigar to light. Castro is laughing his head off, and the generals are laughing at what Castro is saying in Spanish—I don't know whether you'd call it a double-entendre. . . ."

They got it lit. Leifer also got the job done at Mount Fuji, with Japanese gymnast Koji Gushiken posing. "It's December, and it's a national holiday, like our Memorial Day weekend. Everything closes down. We're going to take the picture Saturday or Sunday. Suarez and I get there at four on Friday to rent a cherrypicker. Everything's going to close at five o'clock sharp. We go to the cherrypicker place; the lot's full of all kinds of cherrypickers. The guy there speaks no English. The Time Inc. Japanese bureau guy, Emi, is translating. The rental contract is ready to sign. The Japanese cherrypicker guy looks at me and Suarez. He asks what we're going to do with the cherrypicker. So I draw a little stick figure hanging from the cherrypicker, in front of Mount Fuji. I say, 'This is the cherrypicker, and this is your greatest athlete, Koji Gushiken.' You know the Japanese when they make up their mind. I could see his face changing. Can't hang a man from the cherrypicker; his insurance doesn't cover that. He rips the contract in half, fourths, eighths. . . .

"Emi is arguing with him. But no. No. So Emi called a cousin in Yokohama in the construction business, who drove all night to bring in a cherrypicker from eight hours away.

"Then Gushiken didn't want to get out of his sweats—it's bitter cold. I told him his Chinese counterpart did it and that it was even colder on the Great Wall—appealed to his tough-guy image."

So Gushiken hung thinly clad from the rings suspended from the cherrypicker for half an hour, and Leifer shot twenty rolls or so of film, and the best shot is here in this book in sharp focus.

Also carefully composed. "My adrenaline comes from something inside my head," Leifer says. "My favorite pictures are things that came from my brain, not because I was lucky."

But however much planning is involved, the best sports pictures manage to snag something on the wing, something that comes from inside the athlete. Look at Chinese gymnast Zhou Qiurui springing up fresh and free and tiny and fully extended—even her shadow looks ecstatic, rigorously ecstatic if that is possible, on the ancient cold stones of the Great Wall.

Camera comes from the Latin for vaulted room, an arched chamber. Many of these photographs, rectangular as they are, describe high arcs. Michael Jordan up next to the basket according to his personal law of physics, a cheerleader at the top of her game, a speedboat vaulting the waves, Daley Thompson envisioning trajectory with javelin and eyes.

Even when nothing is surging or leaping in these pictures, they pulse. A closeup of a quarterback beaming semi-toothfully—Terry Bradshaw all over. Martina Navratilova looking arrows at the just-tossed ball she is coiled—arteries a'poppin'—to serve. Bear Bryant compressing rock-'em, sock-'em thinking into strokes of chalk.

But the picture that gives me the biggest lift is the one of Zhou Qiurui. The Wall itself, it goes without saying, is an impressive sight. The Wall shambles agedly off into the background, however, behind the arched Chinese gymnast's spark, as she has focused it in her spring and as Leifer has managed to catch it on the hearth of his camera. Her leap stands a chance now of lasting as long as the Wall.

Roy Blount, Jr.

21

THE PHOTOGRAPHS

WITH COMMENTARY BY

NEIL LEIFER

Eric and Beth Heiden
Davos, Switzerland
January 1980

Two-man luge, four-man bobsled, 90-meter ski jump, speed skating, and downhill skiing—these are sports most American photographers don't often have the opportunity to shoot. Every four years the Olympics provides the chance, and I go after it. I've covered seven Winter Games, and in every case the challenge to produce exciting images is matched by the beauty of these curious sports. The shots always seem fresh, and photographing these events is more fun than work. While the following pictures best show off the spectacle of Olympic competition, there are times when a carefully posed shot—such as the one of Eric and Beth Heiden together—does as much to reveal the drive and determination of these exceptional athletes.

Men's 500-meter speed skating
Winter Olympic Games
Albertville, France
February 1992

Austrian team II
Four-man bobsled
Winter Olympic Games
Albertville, France
February 1992

Unified team
Men's two-seater luge
Winter Olympic Games
Albertville, France
February 1992

Petra Kronberger (Austria)
Downhill skiing
Winter Olympic Games
Calgary, Canada
February 1988

OVERLEAF:
90-meter ski jump
Winter Olympic Games
Calgary, Canada
February 1988

OVERLEAF, LEFT:
Vladimir Artemov (USSR)
All-around gymnastics gold medalist
Summer Olympic Games
Seoul, South Korea
September 1988

OVERLEAF, RIGHT:
Greg Louganis
Springboard and platform gold medalist
Summer Olympic Games
Seoul, South Korea
September 1988

Perfection is most easily studied in a frozen moment. The action occurs so fast it's impossible, unless you're a judge, to pick up the small imperfections. The following three photographs of Yelena Shushunova, Vladimir Artemov, and Greg Louganis clearly show why each was an Olympic gold medalist.

Ski jumper
Sapporo, Japan
February 1971

Yelena Shushunova (USSR)
All-around gymnastics gold medalist
Summer Olympic Games
Seoul, South Korea
September 1988

Paul "Bear" Bryant
University of Alabama football coach
Tuscaloosa, Alabama
September 1980

This is legendary football coach Bear Bryant of the University of Alabama—one tough guy. That is, until you walked into his home and met Mrs. Bryant. It was obvious who wore the pants around the house. I found it very amusing.

What I remember most is how considerate Bryant was. He invited me to his home for dinner, where he asked me about my life and what I had been doing. He seemed genuinely interested, so I told him I had recently directed a film that was premiering soon in London. I next saw Bryant about three months later, when Alabama clinched the national championship at the Sugar Bowl. He noticed me rushing onto the crowded field to take his picture, stopped to shake my hand, and amazed me by asking, "How did it go?"

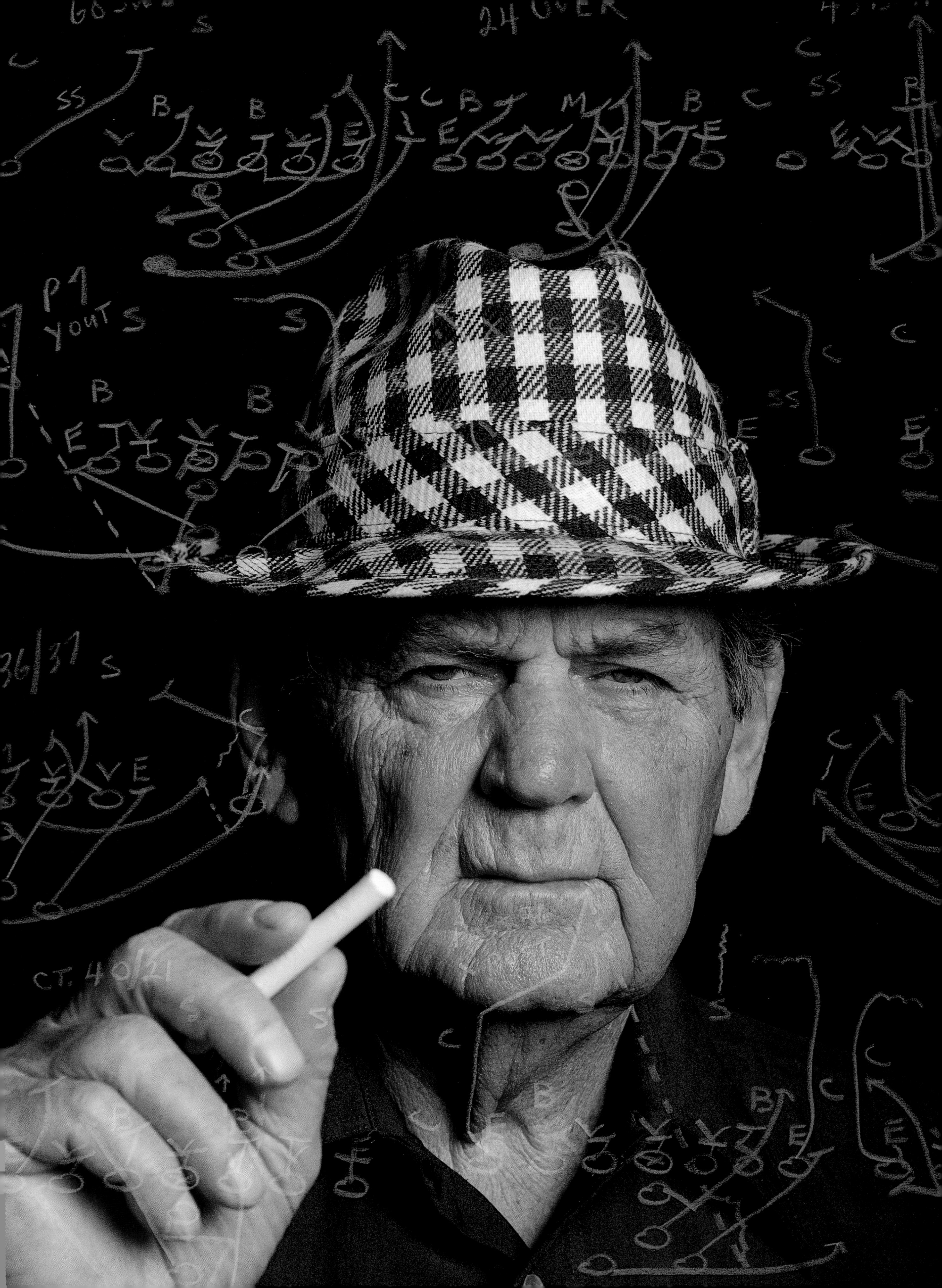
24 OVER
P1
YOUTS
36/37
CT. 40/21

Bob Brown
Oakland Raiders
Oakland, California
October 1971

The sidelines in football are always rewarding photographically. It's the only time the players take off their helmets, which gives you the chance to measure the emotion of the game on their faces. Terry Bradshaw certainly had a lot to smile about during the Pittsburgh Steelers' glory years and four Super Bowl wins, even if he didn't have all his teeth.

Terry Bradshaw
Pittsburgh Steelers
Pittsburgh, Pennsylvania
November 1971

Lawrence Taylor
New York Giants
East Rutherford, New Jersey
December 1991

Florida A&M University marching band
Washington, D.C.
November 1989

OVERLEAF:
Army cheerleaders
West Point, New York
November 1989

Jim Kelly
Buffalo Bills vs. New York Jets
Rich Stadium
Orchard Park, New York
December 1991

Warren Moon
Houston Oilers vs. New York Giants
Giants Stadium
East Rutherford, New Jersey
December 1991

These shots of Jim Kelly and Warren Moon reflect pro football in the nineties: astroturf and spotless uniforms. You'd never know it was the fourth quarter. The following pages of Jim Brown charging through the mud and a battered-looking Sam Huff—well, this is football as I prefer it.

PRECEDING:
Jim Brown
Cleveland Browns vs. San Francisco 49ers
Kezar Stadium
San Francisco, California
December 1962

Cleveland Browns vs. San Francisco 49ers
Kezar Stadium
San Francisco, California
December 1962

Sam Huff
New York Giants
Bronx, New York
November 1962

Jackie Joyner-Kersee
Los Angeles, California
April 1988

Kazushito Manabe (Japan)
Weightlifting
Summer Olympic Games
Seoul, South Korea
September 1988

Daley Thompson (Britain)
Decathlon gold medalist
Summer Olympic Games
Los Angeles, California
August 1984

Jackie Joyner-Kersee
Heptathlon gold medalist
Summer Olympic Games
Seoul, South Korea
September 1988

RIGHT AND OVERLEAF:
Carl Lewis
Houston, Texas
April 1988

For the picture on the following spread I had originally planned to take an action shot of Carl Lewis bursting out of the blocks. But sometimes the setting dictates the shot. The empty stands and the lines of the track made me think of the moment at the beginning of a race when the runner kneels down, hands on the tape, and slowly gazes down the length of the lane. Sometimes the entire race can depend on that quiet time. Carl, who has had many such moments, knew exactly what I wanted.

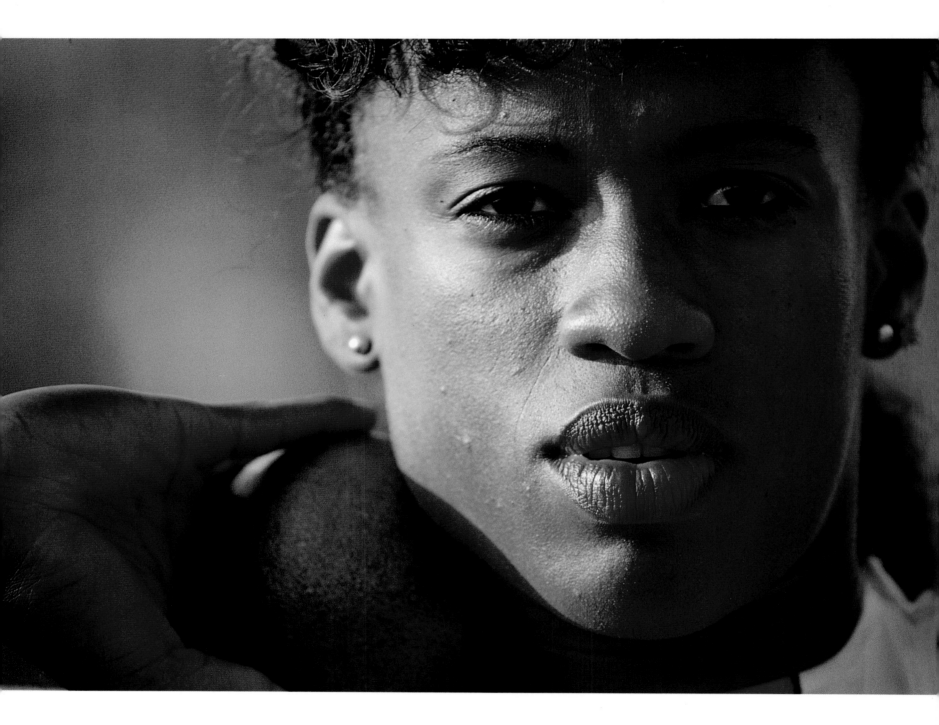

Jackie Joyner-Kersee
Los Angeles, California
April 1988

Start of the New York City Marathon
Verrazano-Narrows Bridge
Brooklyn, New York
November 1991

ABOVE AND OVERLEAF:
New York City Marathon
Brooklyn, New York
November 1991

More often than not, a sports photographer has the best seat in the house. For the New York City Marathon that seat turned out to be in a helicopter. It was great for avoiding the incredible crush of traffic on the ground.

But while I had one eye on my viewfinder, the other was nervously looking out for the twelve helicopters flying around me—carrying other photographers who'd had the same bright idea.

63

USA vs. USSR
Ice hockey
Winter Olympic Games
Calgary, Canada
February 1988

Philadelphia Flyers vs. Boston Bruins
The Spectrum
Philadelphia, Pennsylvania
April 1977

OVERLEAF:
Women's collegiate lacrosse
University of Maryland vs. Penn State University
April 1978

I had never seen a women's lacrosse match before this one
between Maryland and Penn State. Just before the start, as I
was setting up my cameras, I noticed that the women were
putting rubber guards in their mouths. I had only known
boxers to use them (although hockey players certainly
should). Once the game began and they proceeded to beat
the living daylights out of each other, I understood. Unless
you like toothless smiles, it makes a lot of sense.

Roberto Bettega
Italy vs. West Germany
World Cup soccer
Argentina
June 1978

PRECEDING, LEFT:
Women's collegiate softball
Omaha, Nebraska
May 1978

PRECEDING, RIGHT:
Women's collegiate rugby
University of Colorado
Boulder, Colorado
May 1978

72

The Netherlands vs. Italy
World Cup soccer
Argentina
June 1978

It is difficult to imagine the hysteria gener-
ated by the World Cup soccer tournament.
Even more than the Olympics, it is the
world's greatest athletic showdown. It is
especially exciting when the host nation
wins, as Argentina did when I covered the
tournament in 1978. Every victory became a
cause for a national holiday. The fans were
so obsessed the referee had more protection
than the president of the country.

Brazil vs. Austria
World Cup soccer
Argentina
June 1978

Janet Evans
400-meter freestyle
gold medalist
Summer Olympic Games
Seoul, South Korea
September 1988

White-water canoe race
Hudson River Derby
New York, New York
May 1978

White-water rafting
Hudson River Derby
New York, New York
May 1978

Motorboat race
Long Beach to San Francisco, California
October 1966

OVERLEAF:
Eight-oared shell final
Summer Olympic Games
Los Angeles, California
August 1984

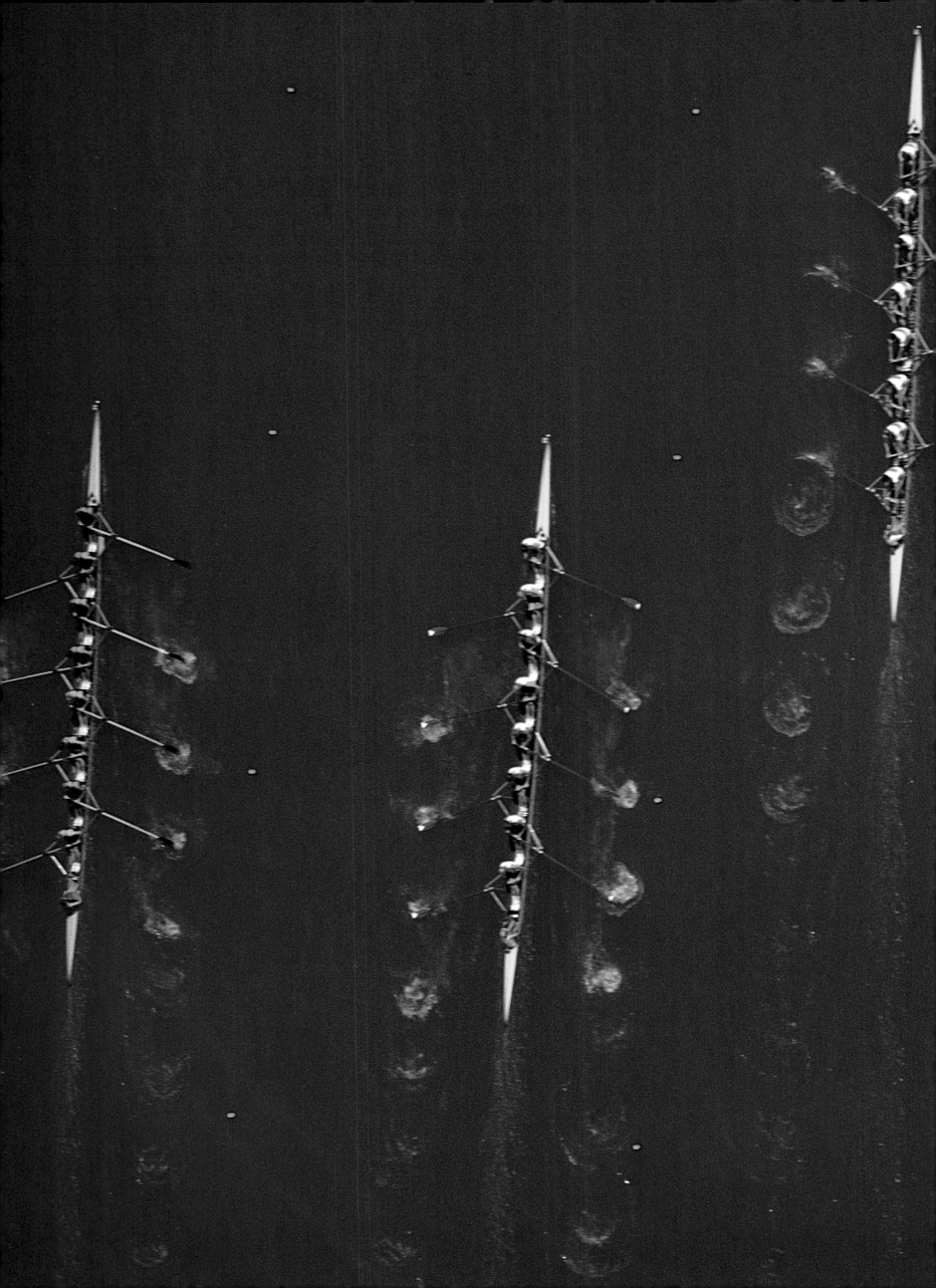

Arnold Palmer
U.S. Open
San Francisco, California
June 1966

ABOVE AND OVERLEAF:
Jack Nicklaus
The Masters
Augusta, Georgia
March 1972 and April 1975

While luck is important in sports photography, sometimes the perfect image is literally handed to you—such as Jack Nicklaus playing in the Masters at Augusta.

The man, the sport, and the magnificent setting simply belong together. As for the reflection in the pond, I was fortunate in that his ball landed precisely where I wanted it.

Bjorn Borg
Davis Cup
Sweden
June 1980

Martina Navratilova
U.S. Open
Flushing, New York
September 1984

Carl Lewis
Long jump gold medalist
Summer Olympic Games
Los Angeles, California
August 1984

One of the greatest mistakes I ever made was missing Bob Beamon's record-setting long jump at the 1968 Olympics in Mexico City. Along with the other photographers, I was on the other side of the field focusing on Lee Evans in the 400-meter final when Beamon jumped 29 feet, 2½ inches and extended the previous mark by an astounding 21¾ inches. Since there can be as many as six rounds in the long jump, we figured we'd get another shot later, but it started to rain and Beamon made only one more attempt before deciding to pass on the rest.

So when Carl Lewis came to the 1984 Los Angeles Games and was scheduled to participate in the 100 meters, the 200 meters, and the relay in addition to the long jump, I figured I'd better be right there at the pit waiting for him. At that point, he was undefeated in thirty-six straight competitions, dating back to 1981. True to form, Lewis nailed the gold medal on his first jump.

OVERLEAF:
Kipkoech and Charles Cheruiyot
Kenyan Olympic runners
Nanyuki, Kenya
March 1984

Maricica Puică (Romania)
3,000-meter run gold medalist
Summer Olympic Games
Los Angeles, California
August 1984

The 3,000-meter final at the Los Angeles Games was supposed to be a duel between Mary Decker and Zola Budd. When Decker tripped over Budd's feet and crashed to the track, the story of the race became the look of pain on Decker's face and the shattering of her dream to finally win an Olympic gold medal. I thought about running over to where she fell, but having already missed the moment, I decided to hold my position at the finish line, where the other story unfolded: Maricica Puică, with a golden halo for a crown, was the winner.

Florence Griffith-Joyner
200-meter dash gold medalist
Summer Olympic Games
Seoul, South Korea
September 1988

Florence Griffith-Joyner
Summer Olympic Games
Seoul, South Korea
September 1988

For many athletes, the pressure to win results
in a cold determination and a lack of emotion. You certainly couldn't say that about
Flo-Jo. While winning the 100 and 200
meters, she spread her arms out wide at the
finish line, then fell to her knees to thank
God, embraced her husband, circled the
track flag in hand, and let it all out on the
victory stand.

Theresa Spivey
Side horse vault
Summer Olympic Games
Seoul, South Korea
September 1988

Bart Conner
Horizontal bar
Summer Olympic Games
Los Angeles, California
August 1984

Zhou Qiurui
Chinese Olympic gymnast
Great Wall, China
December 1983

During my trip to China, I was determined to photograph the country's best gymnasts on the Great Wall. The Chinese officials insisted it was too far from Beijing, where the athletes were training. Besides, they said, there was a very famous temple in the city that all the other photographers used as their background. There was even a replica of this temple at Disneyland, it was so famous. I persisted and eventually got my way. Unfortunately, it was so cold on the Wall I never could convince the athletes to take off their sweats and pose in their competition uniforms.

At Mount Fuji (overleaf), when Koji Gushiken objected to the cold and wanted to pose in his sweats, I played a little with the truth. I told him that his Chinese competitors had posed in even colder temperatures. Gushiken's pride convinced him that if the Chinese gymnasts could do it, then so could he. Off came the sweats.

FOLLOWING PAGES:

Koji Gushiken
Japanese Olympic gymnast
Mount Fuji, Japan
November 1983

Sergei Bubka (USSR)
Pole vault gold medalist
Summer Olympic Games
Seoul, South Korea
September 1988

Patrick Ortlieb (Austria)
Downhill gold medalist
Winter Olympic Games
Albertville, France
February 1992

OPPOSITE TOP:
Bill Johnson
Downhill gold medalist
Winter Olympic Games
Sarajevo, Yugoslavia
February 1984

OPPOSITE BOTTOM:
Pirmin Zurbriggen (Switzerland)
Downhill gold medalist
Winter Olympic Games
Calgary, Canada
February 1988

These photographs of Olympic downhill champs Johnson, Zurbriggen, and Ortlieb were taken at spots on the course where I couldn't see the skiers until they were airborne. I kept my camera pointed at the line I knew the top skiers were taking and listened for the crowd's reaction as each racer approached the bump. In a flash the skier shot in and out of the frame, while I prayed the pictures would turn out as well as they did.

Rosi Mittermaier (West Germany)
Slalom gold medalist
Winter Olympic Games
Innsbruck, Austria
February 1976

OVERLEAF:
The Face of Bellevarde
Downhill ski course at Val-d'Isère
Winter Olympic Games
Albertville, France
February 1992

Kristi Yamaguchi
Orlando, Florida
January 1992

I first photographed Kristi Yamaguchi just after she skated a near flawless performance to win the U.S. Nationals in 1992. She celebrated well into the night, along with the rest of the skaters who had qualified for the Olympic team, then posed for me the next day. After falling on her second or third jump, a very embarrassed Kristi got up, apologized, and, with the same grace that made her a champion, executed a series of perfect jumps.

OVERLEAF:
Kristi Yamaguchi
Figure skating gold medalist
Winter Olympic Games
Albertville, France
February 1992

Isabelle Brasseur and Lloyd Eisler (Canada)
Pairs figure skating bronze medalists
Winter Olympic Games
Albertville, France
February 1992

Elena Betchke and Denis Petrov (Unified team)
Pairs figure skating silver medalists
Winter Olympic Games
Albertville, France
February 1992

Natalia Michkouteniok and Artour Dmitriev
(Unified team)
Pairs figure skating gold medalists
Winter Olympic Games
Albertville, France
February 1992

Joe Fargis riding Mill Pearl
Bridgehampton, New York
June 1988

Bill Hartack aboard Majestic Prince
Santa Anita Derby
Arcadia, California
March 1969

Chris McCarron aboard Alysheba
Breeders' Cup Classic
Churchill Downs
Louisville, Kentucky
November 1988

Often the worst possible conditions turn into
the most dramatic photo opportunities. The
Breeders' Cup is a race usually run under
gloriously sunny skies. This would have been
just another shot of the horses crossing the
wire if not for the rain-soaked track, the
heavy black sky, and the huge flood lights
needed for the photo finish.

Steve Cauthen
Aqueduct Racetrack
Ozone Park, New York
May 1978

Bill Shoemaker
Breeders' Cup
Hollywood Park
Los Angeles, California
November 1984

Breeders' Cup
Hollywood Park
Los Angeles, California
November 1984

Peter Revson
Indy 500
Indianapolis, Indiana
May 1973

OVERLEAF:
Red Mountain motorcycle race
Mojave Desert, California
March 1975

I have always considered baseball the most difficult sport to photograph. Apart from the cliché images of a double play at second base, a pitcher in motion, or a play at home plate, there's not a lot of intense action. Even the players' faces are generally held in fixed concentration, only occasionally revealing an outburst of emotion. Baseball is a game of moments, and you have to be ready for the play that could break the game open.

Showing a famous athlete at a key moment in an important game can make for a great image. The picture on page 142, taken in the ninth inning of the final playoff game in 1962, shows Willie Mays getting the hit that beat the Dodgers and sent the Giants into the World Series. The scoreboard and the crowd's stunned reaction tell the whole story. I was glad to get the shot, but for an old Brooklyn Dodger fan like me, it was a tough moment.

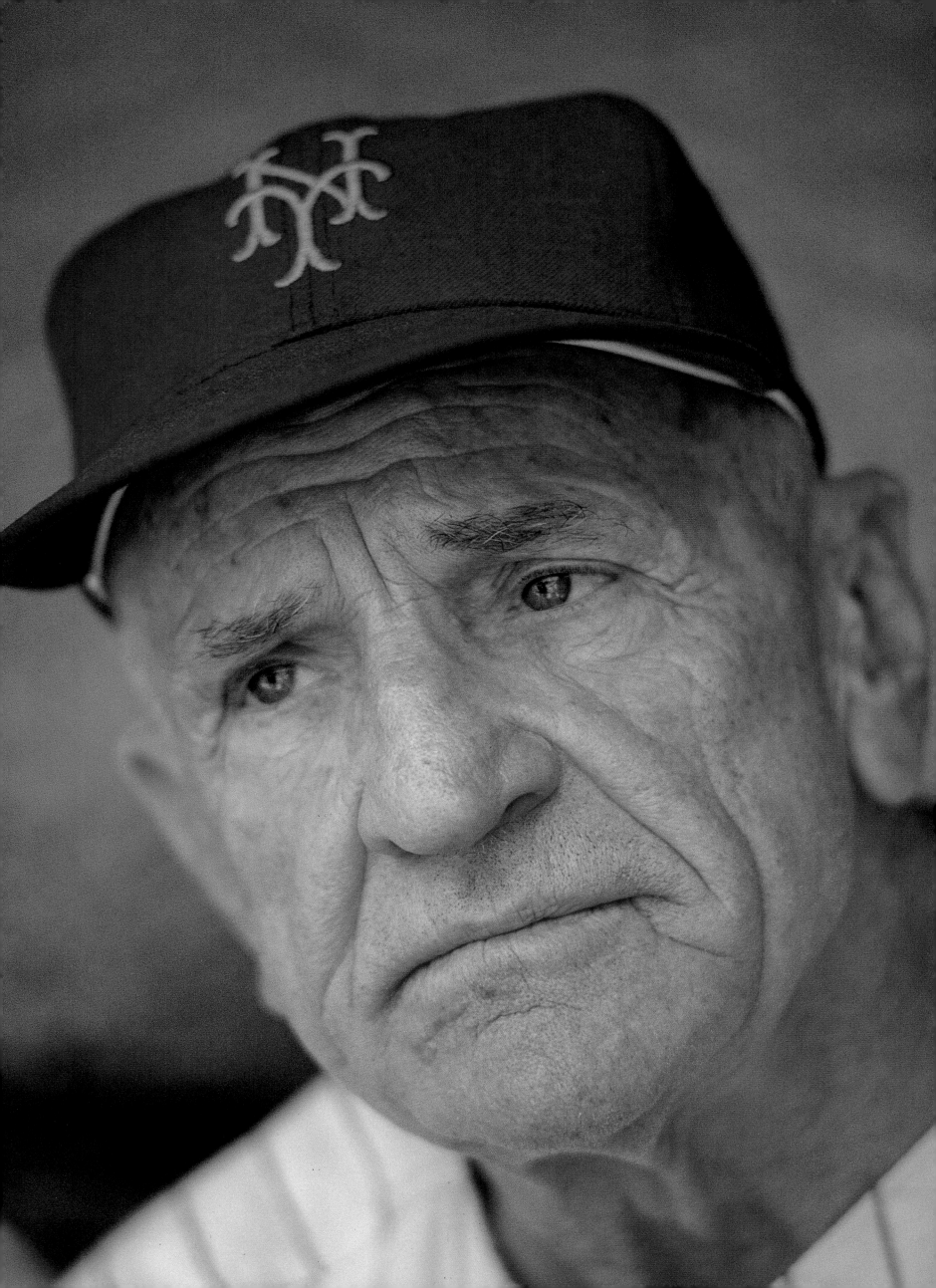

140

Michael Jordan
Chicago Bulls vs. New Jersey Nets
Meadowlands Arena
East Rutherford, New Jersey
December 1991

What Muhammad Ali was to sports photography in the seventies, Michael Jordan is today. Whether he's driving for a layup, dunking the ball, or simply lining up for a foul shot, it's simply impossible to take a bad picture of him.

Earvin "Magic" Johnson
Former Los Angeles Laker
New York, New York
December 1991

The Magic smile—it says everything about
the genuine and winning qualities Magic
Johnson displayed as a player and as a
human being. None would have thought
that the most dramatic moment in his
storied career would have been his an-
nouncement in November 1991 that he had
contracted the virus that causes AIDS and
was retiring from basketball.

Michael Jordan
Chicago Bulls vs. New Jersey Nets
Meadowlands Arena
East Rutherford, New Jersey
December 1991

Earvin "Magic" Johnson
Member of the 1992 U.S. Men's
Olympic Basketball Team
Beverly Hills, California
May 1992

Robert Parish and Patrick Ewing
Boston Celtics vs. New York Knicks
Madison Square Garden
New York, New York
December 1991

Lew Alcindor (later Kareem Abdul-Jabbar)
UCLA vs. University of Dayton
NCAA tournament championship game
Louisville, Kentucky
March 1967

Pete Carril
Princeton University basketball coach
Princeton, New Jersey
March 1990

Though basketball is a game dominated
by big men like Kareem Abdul-Jabbar,
Princeton coach Pete Carril shows there's
a place in the sport for the little guy. He
was a favorite subject of mine, as any
photographer 5 feet, 6 inches or shorter
would understand.

Muhammad Ali vs. Sonny Liston
Heavyweight title fight
Lewiston, Maine
May 1965

This picture of Muhammad Ali vs. Sonny Liston
in Lewiston shows the way boxing used to be: a
world championship fight in a small-town arena
and no beer advertisements on the canvas. By
the time the main event rolled around, a heavy
blue cloud of smoke hung over the ring and cast
a soft haze over the fighters.

You can't smoke anymore, and the arenas have
given way to the brightly lit palaces of Las Vegas
and Atlantic City, where Sugar Ray Leonard and
Mike Tyson made their fortunes. As the young-
est heavyweight champion ever at the age of
twenty, Tyson attracted media attention like no
one since Ali. But unlike Ali, Tyson rarely used
the camera to his advantage. Ali may be long
retired, but in my book he was, and always will
be, the Greatest.

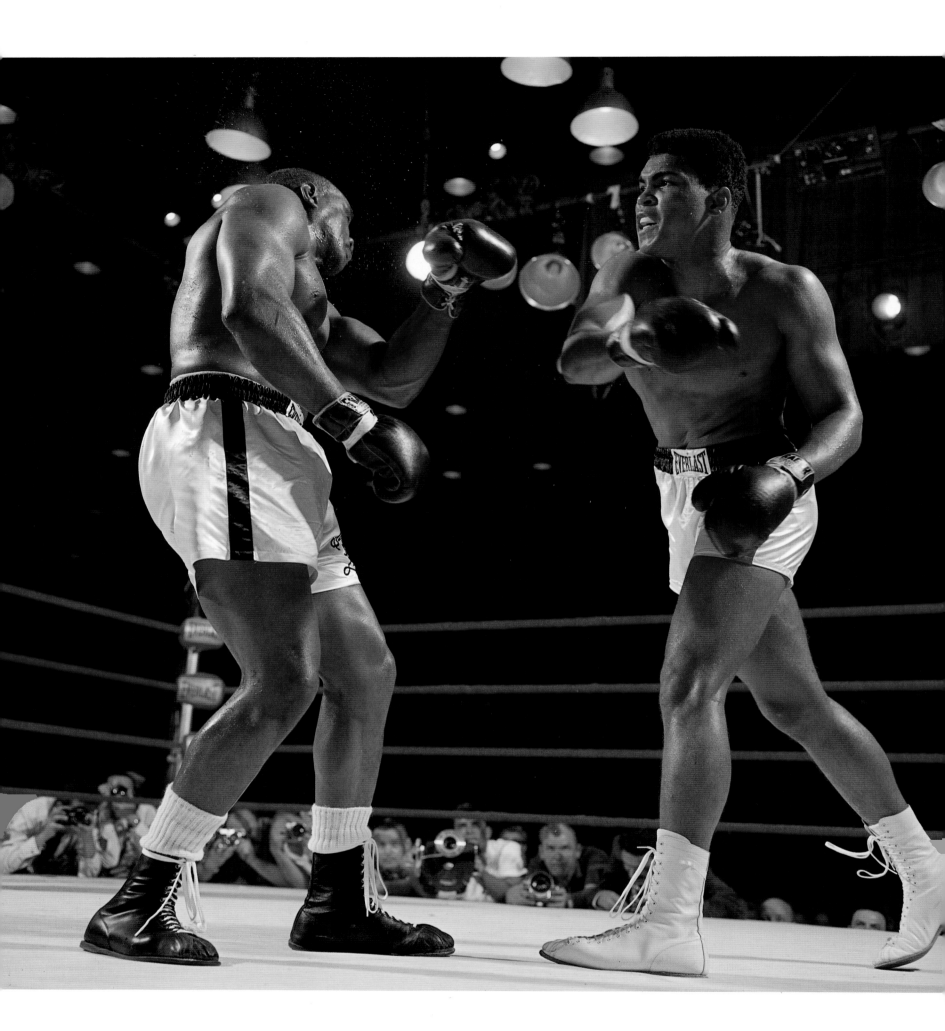

Sonny Liston vs. Cassius Clay (later
Muhammad Ali)
Heavyweight title fight
Miami, Florida
February 1964

Muhammad Ali
New York, New York
January 1992

OVERLEAF:
Mike Tyson vs. Trevor Berbick
Heavyweight title fight
Las Vegas, Nevada
November 1986

George Foreman
Houston, Texas
April 1991

Mike Tyson
Atlantic City, New Jersey
June 1988

George Foreman
Heavyweight title fight vs. Evander Holyfield
Atlantic City, New Jersey
April 1991

Mike Tyson
Atlantic City, New Jersey
June 1988

Evander Holyfield with Lou Duva
Heavyweight title fight vs. George Foreman
Atlantic City, New Jersey
April 1991

Don King
Boxing promoter
Las Vegas, Nevada
February 1989

Sugar Ray Leonard with Angelo Dundee
Welterweight title fight vs. Thomas Hearns
Las Vegas, Nevada
September 1981

OPPOSITE TOP:
Evander Holyfield vs. George Foreman
Heavyweight title fight
Atlantic City, New Jersey
April 1991

OPPOSITE BOTTOM:
Sugar Ray Leonard vs. Roberto Duran
Welterweight title fight
Montreal, Canada
June 1980

Sugar Ray Leonard
Welterweight title fight vs. Roberto Duran
New Orleans, Louisiana
November 1980

FOLLOWING PAGES:

Matt Cetlinski, Doug Gjertsen, Troy Dalbey
4 x 200-meter freestyle gold medalists
Summer Olympic Games
Seoul, South Korea
September 1988

Bonnie Blair
500-meter speed skating gold medalist
Winter Olympic Games
Calgary, Canada
February 1988

Bonnie Blair
500-meter speed skating gold medalist
Winter Olympic Games
Albertville, France
February 1992

Janet Evans
800-meter freestyle gold medalist
Summer Olympic Games
Seoul, South Korea
September 1988

Mary Lou Retton
All-around gymnastics gold medalist
Summer Olympic Games
Los Angeles, California
August 1984

Greg Louganis, Tan Liangde (China),
Li Deliang (China)
Springboard gold, silver, and bronze
medalists, respectively
Summer Olympic Games
Seoul, South Korea
September 1988

Carl Lewis
Statue of Liberty
New York, New York
September 1983

ACKNOWLEDGMENTS

The creation of this book I owe to the same team that produced my first book of sports photographs in 1978. Back then, Lena Tabori, as vice president of marketing at Harry N. Abrams, first saw and championed my work. Now, as publisher of Collins in San Francisco, she has done so again. Both times, much to my good fortune, she has made it possible for me to collaborate with designer Nai Chang. Together their efforts have resulted in two books that are among my proudest accomplishments.

In the fourteen years between these books, many people have helped me, most of all my mom, who I think is the very best, and my two wonderful children, Corey and Jodi, who have accepted my life of frequent travel and long periods on the road. *Time* magazine picture editors Arnold Drapkin and Michele Stephenson gave me all the right assignments; art directors Walter Bernard, Rudy Hoglund, and Tom Bentkowski always made my pictures look just right on the page; and *Time's* former managing editor Ray Cave was and continues to be my rabbi and valued friend. Ray, and the late Andre Laguerre, *Sports Illustrated's* managing editor from 1960 to 1974, are the two greatest editors I have known.

For their endless and solid support, thanks to Pat Ryan, former managing editor of *Life* magazine; editors Frank Deford and Rob Fleder, from my stint at *The National Sports Daily*; talented assistants, including Tony Suarez, Jimmy Keyser, and Richard Kosters; and unsung heroes such as Chris Christopoulos, Carmen Romanelli, Hans Kohl, Mike Miller, and Mel Levine.

As for the people who contributed to this book, I am grateful to Heinz Kluetmeier, Karen Mullarkey, George Washington, Dorothy Affa, Kevin McVea, Jeremy Schaap, Ron Meyerson, Vivette Porges, Kim Evans, Katharine Kim, Steve Fine, Cecilia Bohan, Frank Micelotta, Manny Millan, Nat Butler, Noran Trottman, Rachel Somer, Hiro Clark, and Jennifer Downing. Thanks also to Tom Hauser, whose guidance was invaluable, and especially to writers Lance Morrow and Roy Blount, Jr., who have flattered me with their words.

Last but not least, I thank Daniel Cohen, my photographic assistant for the past three and a half years and the incomparable supervisor of my picture collection.

Opening ceremony
Winter Olympic Games
Calgary, Canada
February 3, 1988

FOLLOWING PAGES:

Closing ceremony
Summer Olympic Games
Seoul, South Korea
October 2, 1988

Closing ceremony
Winter Olympic Games
Albertville, France
February 23, 1992

LAST PAGE:

Vladimir Artemov (USSR), Valery Lyukin
(USSR), Dmitri Bilozerchev (USSR)
All-around gold, silver, and bronze
medalists, respectively
Summer Olympic Games
Seoul, South Korea
September 1988

179